# Crafts for Kids Who Are
## LEARNING ABOUT

# FARM ANIMALS

## To Sue, who loves all animals

Text copyright © 2007 by Kathy Ross

Illustrations © 2007 by MIllbrook Press, Inc.

Millbrook Press, Inc.
A division of Lerner Publishing Group
241 First Avenue North
Minneapolis, MN 55401 U.S.A.

Website address: www.lernerbooks.com

Library of Congress Cataloging-in-Publication Data

Ross, Kathy (Katharine Reynolds), 1948–
    Farm animals / Kathy Ross, illustrated by Jan Barger.
        p.    cm.
    (Crafts for kids who are learning about)
        ISBN-13: 978–0–8225–6366–2 (lib. bdg. : alk. paper)
        ISBN-10: 0–8225–6366–5 (lib. bdg. : alk. paper)
        1. Handicraft — Juvenile literature. 2. Animals — Juvenile literature.
    I. Barger, Jan, 1948- II. Title.
    TT160.R7124 2007
    745.5—dc22                                    2005036257

Manufactured in the United States of America
1  2  3  4  5  6 – JR – 12  11  10  09  08  07

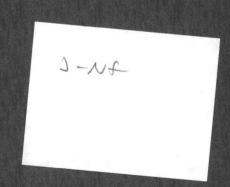

## Crafts for Kids Who Are
# LEARNING ABOUT
# FARM
# ANIMALS

## KATHY ROSS

### Illustrated by Jan Barger

**M** Millbrook Press

Minneapolis

# Table of Contents

Friendly Farmer Puppet 6

Old MacDonald's Barn 8

Crow Finger Puppet 10

Scarecrow Hat 12

T for Tractor 15

Thimble Field Mouse 16

Barn Cat 18

Boa Duck 20

Floating Ducklings 22

Egg-Laying Chicken 23

Rooster Favor  26

Cow Tissue Dispenser  29

Goosey Gander Pin  32

Flower Turkey Corsage  34

Rabbit Ears  36

Farm Dog  38

Bow Sheep  40

Goat Chips Clip  42

Hungry Piggy Puppet  44

Horse Magnet  46

# Friendly Farmer Puppet

The farmer takes care of the animals on the farm.

## Here is what you need:

two craft sticks

two wiggle eyes

ruler

brown bump chenille stem

scissors

sturdy rubber band

wooden tongue depressor stick

white craft glue

permanent markers

## Here is what you do:

1. Break a piece off the end of one of the craft sticks about 2½ inches (6.5 cm) long to use for the hat brim. Use the scissors to trim the broken end, and round off the corners so it matches the uncut ends.

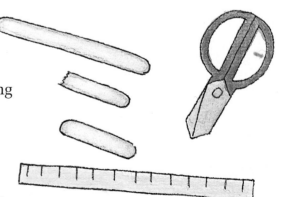

**2.** Glue the stick across the wooden tongue depressor, about 1 inch (2.5 cm) from the top to make the brim of a hat.

**3.** Glue the two wiggle eyes to the tongue depressor just below the brim.

**4.** Break a 1-inch (2.5-cm) piece off the leftover end of the craft stick for the nose. Use the scissors to trim and straighten the cut end of the piece.

**5.** Cut one bump from the bump chenille stem. Bend the bump into a U shape for the beard for the farmer. Glue the beard below the wiggle eyes.

**6.** Glue the flat stick nose below the wiggle eyes so that the rounded end of the nose rests on the beard and sticks out from the face.

**7.** Use the rubber band to attach the second craft stick across the back side of the tongue depressor below the head to form arms.

**8.** Use the markers to color the hat and clothing on the farmer.

*To use the friendly farmer puppet, push down on one arm to make the other arm go up in a friendly wave. "Howdy, friend!"*

# Old MacDonald's Barn

The farm animals live in the barn.

## Here is what you need:

small square box with a lid such as jewelry comes in

red poster paint and a paintbrush

Styrofoam tray to work on

scissors

markers

white copy paper

corrugated lightbulb box

white craft glue

large red seed bead

two or more red, fat marker tops

## Here is what you do:

1. Paint the box and the lid red for the barn, and let them dry on the Styrofoam tray.

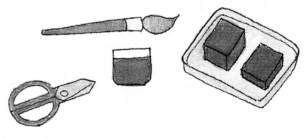

2. Cut a door and roof for the barn from the corrugated cardboard box.

**3.** Place the lid back onto the box, and place the box on its side so the lid faces the front. Glue the door onto the lid, adding the red bead as a doorknob.

**4.** Glue the roof on top of the front part of the barn as shown.

**5.** Glue the two red marker tops, stacked, to one side of the lid for the silo. If you are using a large box, you may have to add a third top to make the silo higher than the barn.

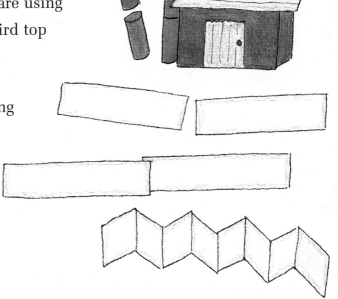

**6.** Cut two white paper strips, making their width a little less than the height of the inside of the box barn. Glue the ends of the two strips together to make one long strip. Fold the strip back and forth, accordion-style, so that it becomes a square that will fit in the box.

**7.** Use the markers to draw a farm animal on each square of the strip.

**8.** Glue the back of the bottom square into the bottom of the box. Glue the back of the top square into the lid of the box.

*You can open up the barn and see all the animals on Old MacDonald's farm! The barn will stand when closed and when opened. Ee-i-ee-i-o!*

9

# Crow Finger Puppet

The crows love to eat the farmer's corn!

## Here is what you need:

two small wiggle eyes

black and orange permanent markers

three fabric-type bandages

white craft glue

## Here is what you do:

1. Peel the paper from one side of one of the bandages. Curl the sticky end of the bandage by folding it over on itself to form the beak for the crow. (Do not remove the paper from the other end of the bandage, which will form the tail of the crow.)

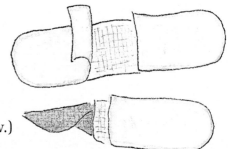

**2.** Use the orange marker to color the beak.

**3.** Peel the paper off both sides of the remaining two bandages. Stick the remaining two bandages together with the center of the first bandage between them. The two bandages will form the wings for the crow.

**4.** Color the bandage crow with the black marker.

**5.** Glue the two wiggle eyes to the head of the crow, just behind the orange beak.

*To use the crow puppet, slip your finger between the two padded sections of the bandage at the center of the crow. Caw! Caw!*

# Scarecrow Hat

The farmer makes a scarecrow to try to keep the crows from eating the corn.

## Here is what you need:

two party hats

ruler

white craft glue

3-inch (8-cm) Styrofoam ball

yellow plastic disposable cup

scissors

yellow yarn

masking tape

brown lunch bag

craft ribbon

three buttons

paper clips

red rickrack

# Here is what you do:

1. Flatten one of the party hats, and cut it in half, top to bottom.

2. Roll each side of the hat into a cone, and secure the wrap with glue and masking tape. Put a paper clip over the masking tape on each of the cones until the glue dries. These will be the arms for the scarecrow.

3. Cut about 2 inches (5 cm) off the point of each of the cones.

4. Cut a square piece from the brown lunch bag large enough to cover the Styrofoam ball and hang down enough to tie at the neck.

5. Press the Styrofoam ball onto the point of the second party hat for the head of the scarecrow.

6. Remove the ball from the hat, dip the point of the hat in the glue, and place the ball back over the point of the hat.

7. Cover the ball with glue, and then wrap it in the brown paper. Secure the paper at the neck of the scarecrow by tying it with a piece of craft ribbon. Trim any uneven edges of the bag.

(continued on next page)

**8.** Glue the buttons on the head for the scarecrow's eyes and nose. Glue a piece of the red rickrack on the head for a mouth.

**9.** Cut about 2 inches (5 cm) from the rim of the yellow cup.

**10.** Cut 1-inch (2.5-cm) slits around the cup. Fold the slits out to form the brim of the hat for the scarecrow.

**11.** Tie a piece of ribbon or rickrack trim around the hat for a hatband and secure with glue. Then glue the hat onto the scarecrow's head.

**12.** Glue the ends of the two arms under the brown bag's ruffle on the back of the scarecrow so that the arms stick out on each side of the scarecrow's body.

**13.** Glue yellow yarn strands around the hat, under the brown bag edges at the neck, and coming out of each arm to look like straw.

*Put the scarecrow hat on your head and go find some crows to startle!*

# T for Tractor

A farmer needs a tractor to help with all the work on the farm.

## Here is what you need:

plastic magnetic letter *T*

small, medium, and large buttons

white craft glue

## Here is what you do:

1. Turn the plastic letter *T* on one side. The top of the letter *T* will become the front of the tractor.

2. The button sizes will depend on the size of the plastic letter you use. Glue the largest button to the back of the tractor and the medium-size button to the front of the tractor for the wheels.

3. Glue the small button at an angle on the top part of the tractor for the steering wheel.

*Stick the tractor on your refrigerator.*

# Thimble Field Mouse

When the corn is stored in the barn, the field mice like to come in and nibble on it.

## Here is what you need:

old thimble

ruler

white craft glue

tiny pink pom-pom

two small pink pom-poms

two tiny wiggle eyes

scissors

pink embroidery floss

# Here is what you do:

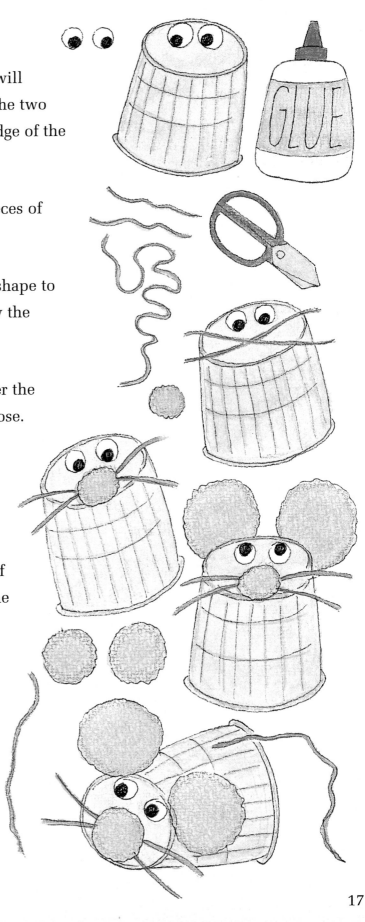

1. The bottom of the thimble will be the face of the mouse. Glue the two wiggle eyes to the bottom top edge of the thimble.

2. Cut two 1-inch (2.5-cm) pieces of the pink floss for whiskers.

3. Glue the whiskers in an X shape to the bottom of the thimble below the eyes.

4. Glue the tiny pom-pom over the center of the whiskers for the nose.

5. Glue the two small pink pom-poms at the edge of the thimble as the mouse's ears.

6. Cut a 2-inch (5-cm) piece of the pink embroidery floss for the tail.

7. Glue the tail to the edge of the thimble behind the ears.

*Maybe you can find enough old thimbles to make a mouse for each finger! Squeak! Squeak!*

# Barn Cat

The farmer's cat helps chase the mice out of the barn.

## Here is what you need:

orange, tan, white, and black faux-fur scraps

cardboard tube

ruler

two wiggle eyes

string

black pom-pom

Styrofoam tray to work on

scissors

white craft glue

clamp clothespins

## Here is what you do:

1. Cut a 4-inch (10-cm) piece off one end of the cardboard tube.

2. Flatten one end of the tube, and cut a V-shaped wedge out of the flattened end, which will leave two triangle-shaped ears.

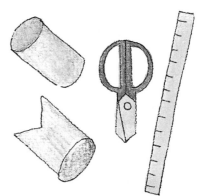

**3.** Glue the front and back sides of the flattened end of the tube together. Secure the glued end of the tube with a clamp clothespin until the glue has dried.

**4.** Cut odd-shaped pieces from the different colors of faux fur.

**5.** Working on the Styrofoam tray, glue the pieces all over the outside of the tube to cover it.

**6.** Cut a 1- by 5-inch (2.5- by 13-cm) piece of fur for the tail. Fold the piece of fur in half so that the long strip makes a tail with fur on both sides. Glue the folded sides together. Use the clamp clothespins to secure the fold until the glue is dry.

**7.** Once the glue is dry, glue the folded tail to the cat.

**8.** Turn the cat around to face front, and glue two wiggle eyes to the tube below the ears.

**9.** Cut two 3-inch (8-cm) pieces of the string for whiskers for the cat.

**10.** Glue the two pieces of string in an X shape below the eyes.

**11.** Glue the black pom-pom over the center of the whiskers for the nose.

*Slip the open end of the tube cat over your fingers, and take him on a hunt for the thimble mouse. Meow, meow!*

19

# Boa Duck

Some farms have ducks.

## Here is what you need:

- white craft feather boa strip
- orange felt scrap
- 12-inch (30-cm) orange pipe cleaner
- scissors
- white craft glue
- orange and white craft ribbon
- two large wiggle eyes
- plastic straw
- ruler

## Here is what you do:

1. Fold the feather boa into an 8-inch-tall (20-cm) figure eight twice. Then trim off the excess.

2. Cut a 12-inch (30-cm) piece of the orange ribbon.

3. Tie the ribbon in a bow around the middle of the figure eight to form the neck of the duck.

4. Cut a 9-inch (23-cm) strip of feather boa.

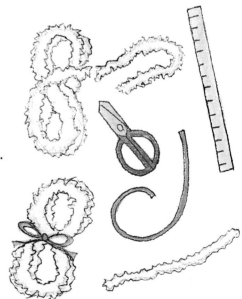

**5.** Thread the feather boa strip through the center of the bottom part of the figure eight to form the wings for the duck. Secure the wings with a dab of glue. Fluff boa feathers to fill in the head and body.

**6.** Fold the orange felt scrap in half, and cut a beak for the duck. Glue the fold of the beak to the head of the duck.

**7.** Glue the two wiggle eyes above the beak.

**8.** Fold the orange pipe cleaner in half. Thread it through the bottom opening of the figure eight, and twist the two ends together at the fold to secure the pipe cleaner.

**9.** Spread the two ends of the pipe cleaner out to form the legs for the duck. Tip the ends forward for feet.

**10.** Cut web feet from the orange felt. Glue a web foot to the end of each leg.

**11.** Cut a 3-inch (8-cm) piece from the straw. Cut a 36-inch (91-cm) and a 30-inch (76-cm) length of the white craft ribbon. Thread the 36-inch piece of ribbon through the piece of straw, and tie each end of the ribbon to the tip of a wing.

**12.** Thread the 30-inch ribbon through the head of the duck, and tie the two ends together above the straw piece.

*Hold on to the straw piece, and take this fuzzy duck for a walk! Quack, Quack!*

# Floating Ducklings

Many farms have ponds where the ducks and baby ducklings can swim.

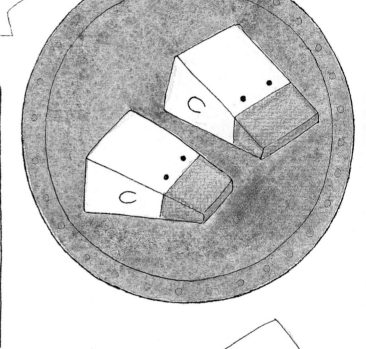

## Here is what you need:

two sponge
makeup
wedges

orange and black
permanent markers

9-inch (23-cm) blue
plastic disposable
plate

water

## Here is what you do:

1. Use the orange marker to color about ½ inch
(1.3 cm) of the pointed end of each sponge
makeup wedge on all sides. This will be
the bill for each duck.

2. Use the black marker to draw a wing on each
side of the sponge and two eyes just above the beak.

3. Pour enough water into the blue plastic plate
to make a small pond for the ducks to float in.

*These ducks would love to join you in the bathtub!*
*Quack, quack!*

# Egg-Laying Chicken

Chickens lay eggs.

## Here is what you need:

red and orange felt scraps

two white disposable dust cloths

plastic egg

two cardboard party hats

three white craft feathers

ruler

old sock with cuff

12-inch (30-cm) orange pipe cleaner

scissors

white craft glue

two small wiggle eyes

(continued on next page)

# Here is what you do:

1. Fold the orange pipe cleaner in half to form the two legs.

2. Cut a 2-inch (5-cm) piece from each end of the pipe cleaner. Wrap a cut piece around each leg about 1 inch (2.5 cm) from the end to form the feet. Bend the feet forward.

3. Cover the outside of the party hat with glue. Wrap the hat with one of the white dust cloths, securing it with more glue where needed.

4. Fold the ends up inside the hat, and glue a second hat inside the first hat to secure the ends.

5. Glue the fold of the pipe cleaner to the bottom center of the chicken.

6. Cut a strip of dust cloth from the second cloth to glue over the center part of the pipe cleaner to secure it.

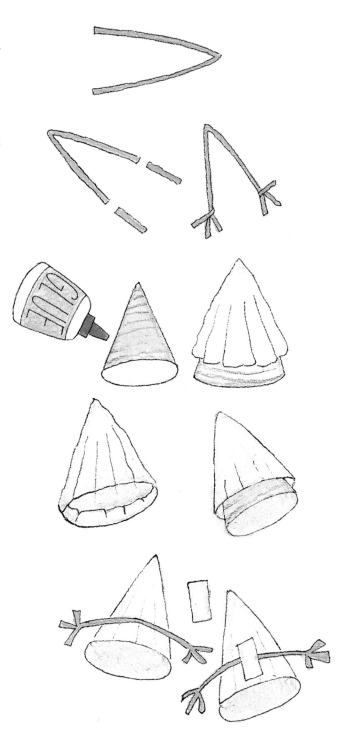

**7.** Cut two triangle beaks from the orange felt scrap. Glue them together over the point of the hat.

**8.** Glue the two wiggle eyes to the top of the head behind the beak.

**9.** Cut a comb from the red felt scrap, and glue it to the top of the head between the eyes.

**10.** Glue a white craft feather to each side of the chicken for wings and on the top back for the tail.

**11.** Cut the cuff from the sock.

**12.** Glue the cuff inside the chicken, without gluing the last 3 inches (8 cm) of the cuff at the open end of the hat.

**13.** Slip the egg inside the sock cuff, inside the chicken.

*Squeeze the chicken gently on each side to make it lay an egg. Cluck, cluck!*

# Rooster Favor

The rooster likes to crow at sunrise.

## Here is what you need:

sixteen 12-inch (30-cm) red, green, brown, and yellow pipe cleaners

two wiggle eyes

white craft glue

ruler

large red rickrack

scissors

brown bump chenille stem

# Here is what you do:

1. Set two of the yellow pipe cleaners aside. Hold the remaining pipe cleaners, and twist the ends together to about a third of the way down to form the head and neck of the rooster.

2. Hold the pipe cleaners about a third of the way from the opposite end. Twist the pipe cleaners together once to secure them. The ends will become the tail of the rooster.

3. Hold the neck and the base of the tail of the rooster, and push toward the middle to bend the center of the pipe cleaners to shape the body.

4. Fold the tail up at the base and then down in the middle.

5. Fold the neck up, and then tip the ends forward to form the head.

6. Wrap a piece of yellow pipe cleaner around the end of the head to make the beak. Glue the two wiggle eyes to the head above the beak.

(continued on next page)

**7.** Cut a 1-inch (2.5-cm) piece of the red rickrack, and glue it to the top of the head for the comb.

**8.** Cut two bumps from the brown bump chenille stem, including the thin end on both ends.

**9.** Thread the bumps through the pipe cleaners at the base of the neck so that a bump sticks up on each side of the neck to form a wing.

**10.** Cut the last yellow pipe cleaner in half to make the legs. Then fold each piece in half.

**11.** Thread each piece through a pipe cleaner at the bottom of the body, and twist the two sides together until the last twist is about ½ inch (1.3 cm) from the ends of the pipe cleaners.

**12.** Fold the two ends forward on each twisted pipe cleaner leg to form the toes.

*To use the rooster as a favor, fill a small plastic bag with colorful candy and tuck the bag inside the body of the rooster. Cock-a-doodle-do!*

# Cow Tissue Dispenser

Cows give us milk.

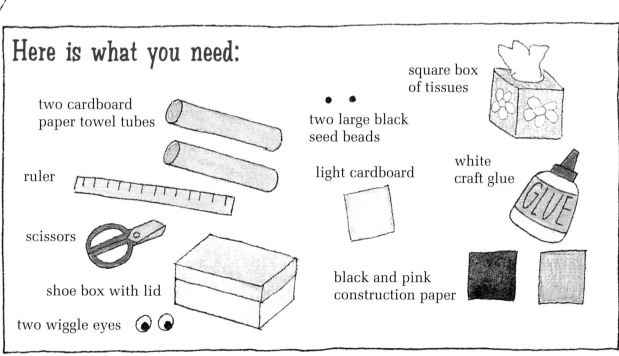

## Here is what you need:

two cardboard paper towel tubes

ruler

scissors

shoe box with lid

two wiggle eyes

two large black seed beads

light cardboard

black and pink construction paper

square box of tissues

white craft glue

GLUE

(continued on next page)

# Here is what you do:

1. Make sure the square tissue box fits inside the shoe box. If it does not, you can cut away half of the back side of the shoe box to make it fit.

2. Cut four 4½-inch (11-cm) pieces from the tubes for legs for the cow, and glue one onto each of the four corners of the lid of the shoe box.

3. Cut an opening in the bottom of the shoe box lid to allow the tissue to be pulled through when the box is placed upside down over the opening.

4. Cut a rectangle body for the cow from the light cardboard that is as wide as the shoe box and tall enough to cover the tissue box and hang another 2 inches (5 cm) down below the shoe box. Glue the body of the cow to the shoe box.

5. Cut an oval-shaped head for the cow from the cardboard and a smaller oval-shaped nose to glue across the bottom of the head for the nose.

6. Cut two ears for the cow from the cardboard, and glue them to the top of the head.

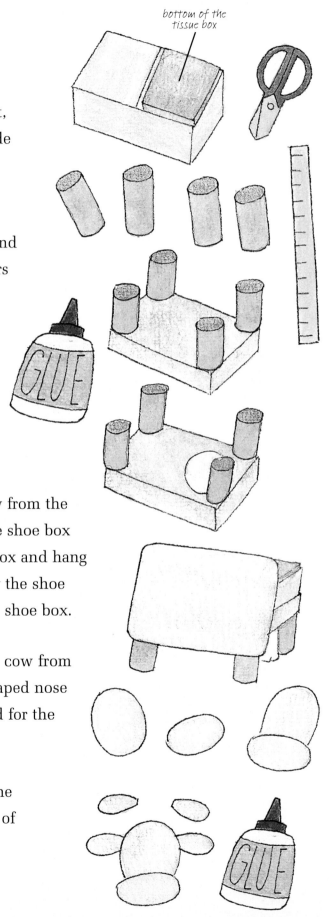

bottom of the tissue box

**7.** Glue the wiggle eyes to the head of the cow.

**8.** Glue the two seed beads to the nose of the cow for the nostrils.

**9.** Glue the head to the cow body, so that about half the head is glued to the body and the other half sticks out beyond it.

**10.** Cut spots for the cow from the black construction paper. Glue the spots to the body and the head of the cow.

**11.** Cut an udder for the cow from the pink paper. Glue the udder to the bottom of the cow in front of the tissue hanging down from the tissue box.

**12.** Cut a tail for the cow from the light cardboard. Glue the tail to the back of the cow.

*The tissue can be pulled down from the bottom of the cow just like you are milking a cow! Moo, moo!*

# Goosey Gander Pin

Some farms have geese.

## Here is what you need:

ruler

two 12-inch (30-cm) white bump chenille stems

one orange bump chenille stem

white craft glue

scissors

safety pin

two black beads

## Here is what you do:

1. Fold the end bump of a white chenille stem forward to shape the head of the goose.

2. Bend the other three bumps back and forth to shape the body.

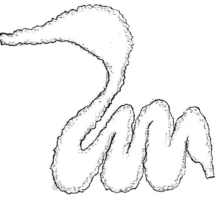

**3.** Wrap the second white bump chenille stem loosely around the outside of the body to make it bigger.

**4.** Cut two orange bumps from the orange chenille stem. Cut half of each bump off.

**5.** Slip the orange piece through the white chenille stems at the bottom center of the body so that half an orange bump hangs down on each side to form the legs and feet. Twist the two sides together at the top of the body to secure the legs.

**6.** Tip each foot forward.

**7.** Fold a 1-inch (2.5-cm) piece of the orange bump chenille over the end of the head to form a beak. Secure with glue. You may need to trim off some of the fuzz from the beak once the glue has dried.

**8.** Glue the two black beads to the head above the beak for the eyes.

**9.** Slip the back of the safety pin through the pipe cleaners at the back of the goose.

*Pin the goose to your coat or shirt collar. Honk! Honk!*

# Flower Turkey Corsage

Some farms raise nothing but turkeys.

## Here is what you need:

two or more different-colored artificial rose-type flowers

orange pipe cleaner

orange bump chenille stem

scissors

white craft glue

two tiny wiggle eyes

safety pin

## Here is what you do:

1. Cut one bump from the orange bump chenille stem with the thin part left on both sides.

**2.** Glue one end of the bump chenille piece into the center of one of the flowers. The flower will be the body of the turkey.

**3.** Fold the top of the bump forward and down to form the head of the turkey.

**4.** Glue the two wiggle eyes on the head of the turkey.

**5.** Bend the orange pipe cleaner in half. Cut a 1-inch (2.5-cm) piece from each end of the pipe cleaner. Wrap a cut piece around each leg about 1 inch (2.5 cm) from the end to form the feet. Bend the feet forward.

**6.** Glue the pipe cleaner legs to the back of the flower, feet pointing forward.

**7.** Cut several large petals from the remaining flowers to use for the tail.

**8.** Glue the petals to the top back of the turkey so that they fan out above the body to shape the tail.

**9.** Attach the safety pin to the back of the turkey so that it can be worn as a corsage.

*This project would make a great gift for someone around Thanksgiving time! Gobble! Gobble!*

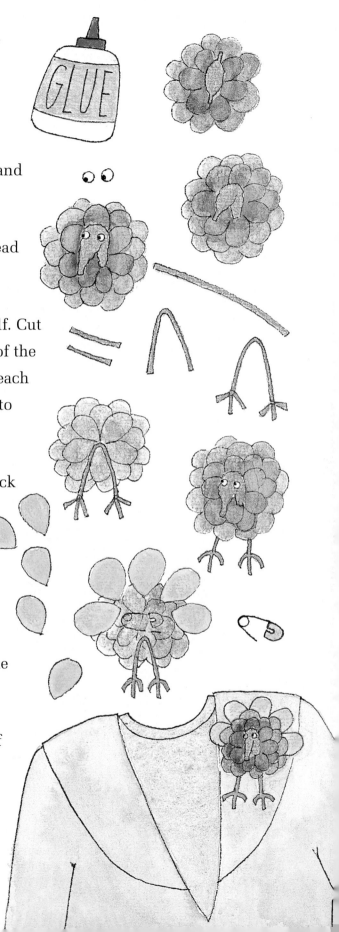

# Rabbit Ears

You might see rabbits on the farm.

## Here is what you need:

pink construction paper

two cardboard party hats with elastic strap

scissors

white craft glue

fiberfill

masking tape

# Here is what you do:

1. Cut two pink triangles from the construction paper so that they are a little smaller than the party hats. Glue them on one side of each hat for the ear liners.

2. Glue bits of fiberfill all over the remainder of each hat to complete the two ears.

3. Use a long strip of the masking tape to tape the two ears together at the base of the ears. Make sure both pink liners are facing forward in the same direction. Place some glue under the strip of tape inside each ear to make the connection extra sturdy.

4. Shorten the chin straps to about half their length by placing a dab of glue over each end of the elastic chin straps. Cover the glue with a small piece of masking tape to secure.

*To wear the bunny ears, place the ears on top of your head and slip a chin strap under each of your own ears. Hop, hop!*

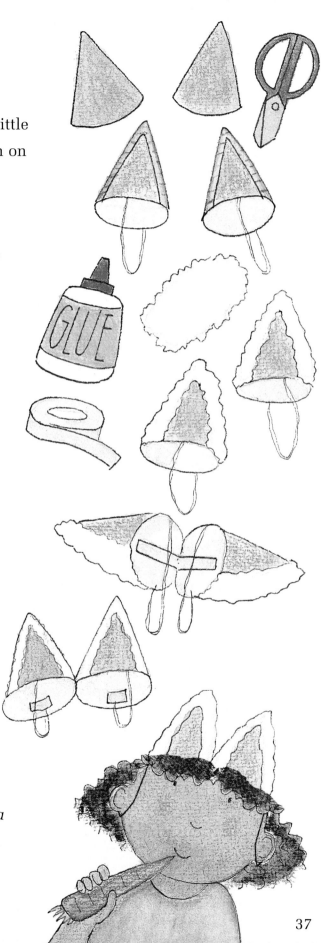

# Farm Dog

Farm dogs help herd the cows and sheep back into the pen or barn.

## Here is what you need:

ruler

cork

scissors

four small brown pom-poms

brown felt scrap

two small wiggle eyes

tiny black pom-pom

white craft glue

GLUE

brown eyelash yarn

# Here is what you do:

1. Cover the cork with glue.

2. Wrap the cork with the brown eyelash yarn until it is entirely covered. Trim off the excess yarn, and press the end into the glued cork to secure.

3. Cut a 3-inch (8-cm) piece of eyelash yarn for a tail. Glue the tail to one end of the wrapped cork.

4. Cut two floppy ears from the brown felt scrap. Glue the ears to the top of the opposite end of the cork.

5. Glue the two wiggle eyes to the end of the cork below the ears.

6. Glue the tiny black pom-pom to the end of the cork under the eyes for the nose.

7. Glue the four brown pom-poms to the bottom of the cork for the legs.

*What a shaggy dog! Woof, woof!*

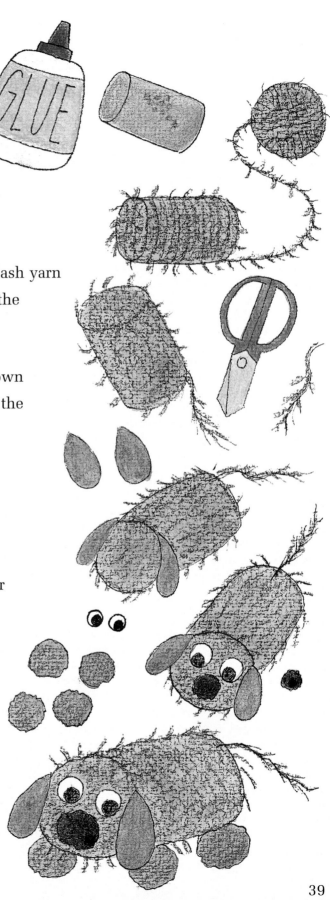

# Bow Sheep

The sheep give us wool for sweaters.

## Here is what you need:

two identical white package bows, the more loops the better

black felt scrap

scissors

two wiggle eyes

white craft glue

tiny pink pom-pom

medium to large black pom-pom and four smaller ones

jingle bell

red craft ribbon

# Here is what you do:

1. Glue the backs of the two white bows together to form a ribbon ball that will be the body for the sheep.

2. The size of the pom-pom you use for the head is going to depend on the size of the bows you choose for the body. Tuck the larger black pom-pom in between the two bows, and secure it with glue.

3. Cut two ears from the black felt scrap, and glue them to the top of the head.

4. Glue the two wiggle eyes to the front of the head below the ears.

5. Glue the pink pom-pom nose below the two wiggle eyes.

6. Thread the jingle bell onto a piece of the red craft ribbon. Tie the ribbon in a bow.

7. Glue the bow to the sheep below the head.

8. Glue the four smaller pom-poms to the bottom of the sheep for the legs.

*Make a flock of sheep in lots of different sizes by using different-size bows for the body. Baa, baa!*

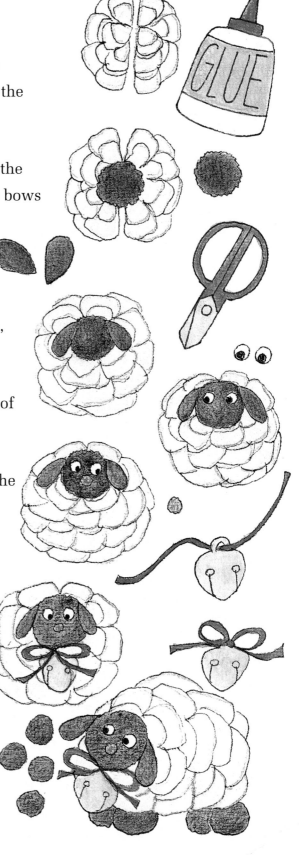

# Goat Chips Clip

Goats like to eat just about anything!

## Here is what you need:

- white and black construction paper
- red felt scrap
- white craft feather fluff
- clamp clothespin
- white craft glue
- scissors
- two white shirt buttons
- two wiggle eyes
- ruler

## Here is what you do:

1. Cut a triangle-shaped head for the goat from the white construction paper that is tall enough to cover one side of the clamp clothespin. Round off the points of the triangle.

2. Glue the head to the clamp clothespin with the narrow end at the end of the clothespin that will open.

**3.** Cut two ears and two horns from the white construction paper.

**4.** Glue the ears to the top sides of the head.

**5.** Glue the horns to the top of the head between the ears.

**6.** Glue the two wiggle eyes to the head below the ears.

**7.** Cut a small nose for the goat from the black construction paper.

**8.** Glue the nose to the bottom of the head.

**9.** Snip some fluff from the craft feather fluff, and glue it behind the chin for the goat's beard.

**10.** Cut a 3-inch (8-cm) shirt shape from the red felt scrap.

**11.** Glue the two buttons on the front of the shirt shape.

**12.** Pinch the clothespin open, and glue the shirt to the inside of the clothespin behind the beard. Be careful not to glue the clothespin shut.

*The goat can be clamped to the top of a chips bag to keep it closed, but I don't know if you can trust him not to eat the chips—and the bag! Chomp, chomp!*

# Hungry Piggy Puppet

Pigs love to eat!

## Here is what you need:

two wiggle eyes

ruler

pink sponge about 3- by 5-inches (8- by 13-cm)

two-holed button

clamp clothespin

scissors

green pipe cleaner

two 1-inch (2.5-cm) red pom-poms

two pink pipe cleaners

white craft glue

## Here is what you do:

1. Cut the pink sponge in half to get two identical 2½- by 3-inch (6- by 8-cm) pieces.

2. Cut a slit in the top of each side of each sponge toward the front to hold the ears.

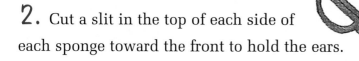

**3.** Stack the two sponges together. Thread one end of one of the pink pipe cleaners down through the slit on one side of both sponges then up through the slit on the other side of both sponges to secure the sponges together.

**4.** Shape the two pipe cleaner ends into triangle-shaped ears for the pig.

**5.** Glue the two wiggle eyes to the top sponge in front of the ears.

**6.** Glue the button to the front edge of the top sponge below the eyes.

**7.** Slide the clamp clothespin in between the two sponges so that the mouth of the pig opens when the clothespin is squeezed. Secure the clothespin with glue, if needed.

**8.** Wrap a 6-inch (15-cm) piece of pink pipe cleaner around the top handle of the clamp clothespin at the back of the pig. Wrap the pipe cleaner tail around your finger to make a spiral.

**9.** Cut two ½-inch (1.3-cm) pieces of green pipe cleaner. Glue a piece of green pipe cleaner into each red pom-pom to make the pom-poms look like apples.

*To use the pig puppet, squeeze the clothespin, opening the pig's mouth to grab a pom-pom apple. Oink, oink!*

# Horse Magnet

Horses can help with the work on the farm and are lots of fun to ride.

## Here is what you need:

three wooden ice-cream spoons

brown paint and a paintbrush

ruler

white craft glue

Styrofoam tray to work on

two large black seed beads

eyelash yarn

scissors

brown paper scrap

two wiggle eyes

piece of sticky-back magnet

## Here is what you do:

1. Paint one side of the three wooden ice-cream spoons brown, and let them dry on the Styrofoam tray.

**2.** Glue the bowl end of two of the spoons together with the handles spread out slightly to form the legs of the horse.

**3.** Glue the bowl end of the last spoon to the top of the legs at an angle, making sure the top is above the other two spoons. This will be the head of the horse.

**4.** Cut two ears for the horse from the brown paper scrap. Glue the two ears to the top of the head.

**5.** Cut a 3-inch (8-cm) piece of the brown eyelash yarn. Glue the yarn around the top of the left side of the head of the horse for the mane.

**6.** Snip some threads from the eyelash yarn to glue between the ears for the forelock.

**7.** Glue the two wiggle eyes to the top part of the head. Glue the two seed beads to the bottom of the head for the nostrils.

**8.** Cut a 3-inch (8-cm) piece of brown eyelash yarn, and glue it to the upper left back of the horse for a tail.

**9.** Press a piece of sticky-back magnet to the back of the horse.

*Make a whole herd of horses in different colors. Neigh, neigh!*

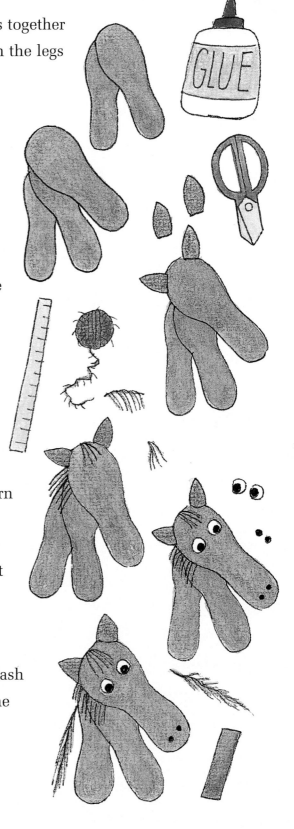

# About the Author and Artist

Thirty years as a teacher and director of nursery school programs have given Kathy Ross extensive experience in guiding young children through crafts projects. Among the more than forty craft books she has written are ***Things to Make for Your Doll***, ***All-Girl Crafts***, ***The Scrapbooker's Idea Book***, ***Girlfriends' Get-together Craft Book***, and the ***All New Holiday Crafts for Kids*** series. You can find out more about Ross's books by visiting her at www.Kathyross.com

Jan Barger, originally from Little Rock, Arkansas, lives in Plumpton, East Sussex, England, with her husband and their cocker spaniel, Tosca. She has written and illustrated a number of children's books and is known for her gentle humor and warm, friendly characters. She also designs greeting cards, sings with the Brighton Festival Chorus, and plays piccolo with the Sinfonia of Arun.

Together, Ross and Barger have written and illustrated the ***Learning Is Fun*** series, as well as earlier books in this series: ***Crafts for Kids Who Are Learning about Community Workers, Crafts for Kids Who Are Learning about Weather,*** and ***Crafts for Kids Who Are Learning about Transportation***.